Purple Sky

A collection of unrequited poems

Pawandeep Kaur

BookLeaf
Publishing

India | USA | UK

Made with ❤ on the BookLeaf Publishing Platform

www.bookleafpub.in

www.bookleafpub.com

Dedication

To

"My Youth, My Twenties"

Acknowledgement

To my mom, family, friends, who pushed me to stages and perform and cheered for me loudest in the room. To all the teachers who believed in me more than I ever could. To my best friends (B & G), To myself who had 20 days but still did this in 2 days. From having a league of poems to unfiltered and unfinished collection of poems, This book is all about unscripted, unrevised and raw emotions, that have helped me stand tall amid all the odds. I am happy I did this. I am filled with unrequited emotions and this collection is an exempt, I hope you enjoy.

Preface

From introducing myself as a writer to finally being one. Its a privilege to be give wings to your dreams yourself. You should not wait for someone to detangle your life, Its YOU, only you can create a path of flowers to walk on amidst the thorns. BTS has always taught me to love myself unconditionally, which is very rare because we are the biggest inhibitory creatures for our dreams, our passion in order to please others regardless of the irresistible guilt we will trap ourself into. The soul purpose of this collection is to feel alive again. This book is my oxygen.

2 minutes

Had the train departed 2 minutes early that
day,
I would have never let go of your hand,
and stopped you from leaving my present,
My present has lost its light,
when there is no you in sight,
No matter how hard I cry,
for how long I cry,
you won't come back to me.
Had the train been canceled that day,
I would have never let go of your hand,
and stopped you from leaving my present,
My present has lost its charm,
when there are no cuddles as warm,
No matter how much I call your name,
for how long I call,
you won't come back to me.

Ifs and Buts

It's okay if you are loud and you are the life of
a party
But
Maybe a conversation in silence with the stars
in the skies.
It's okay if you are affectionate and you feel
every emotion deep down
But
Maybe something platonic that drenches your
soul on its own
It's okay if you love fancy dates and dressing
up for Michelins,
But
Maybe a bowl of ramen by the river or a
movie date with popcorn
It's okay if you plan parties for valentines and
announce it to the whole world,
But
Maybe a rose with a card with words crafted
only for me
It's okay if you love glorifying things and end
up falling for spotlights

But
Maybe finding joy in little things, holding
hands, and watching sun sights.
It's okay if you love video calls and post
everything on your social,
But
Maybe a letter once in a while with
handcrafted feelings on the mail,
It's okay if you don't love K-dramas, and you
wont binge an entire season in one night
But
Maybe holding hands in 12th episode and
crying with me every time I miss a fan sight
It's okay if you love catching flights and
running after duty-free stores at the airport
But
Maybe saving up for a house that will witness
us from black to grey
It's okay if you won't live in my universe and
won't light up my days
But
Maybe you were not meant to be and were
just a part of my midnights.

Golden hour

Birds chirping,
A cup of iced latte in one hand,
and the other holding yours,
under the bridge,
on a rainy day,
echoes of love,
My eyes are on you,
In the realm of forever,
We made promises,
Promises that lasted,
Like the moon and stars,
Paths that crossed,
in the parallel universe,
we will meet,
Meet like our firsts,
in every lifetime.

Falling out of love

I love you,
I love you,
The words that scare me,
the words that made me hate you,
I remember 100 reasons for the words you
said to me,
But I can't make you love me anymore,
I love you
I love you,
The words made me despise you,
The words that me, push away your love,
I remember 100 reasons I was desperate to
make you love me,
But I can't make you love me anymore,
I hate you,
I hate you.

Dressed in vain

I am dressed in sorrow,
with every tear rolling down my cheeks,
marks the times I loved you,
I am dressed in pain,
with every ache in my voice,
marks the times I loved you,
I am dressed in vain,
with every scream that goes out of the room,
marks the times I loved you,
I am dressed in bandages,
with every roll crossing my delicate skin,
marks the times I loved you.
I am dressed in bruises,
with every inch of purple,
marks the time I loved you.

You are my color Orange

You are my color orange,
that gives me hope to breathe,
You are my rainbow,
That pushes me to shine the brightest,
on my gloomy days,
Like a sun pushing the clouds away,
on rainy days,
You are my hope, my sunshine,
that finds its way to return to me, my home,
You are my color orange,
that lifts my spirits,
making my dark days the hits,
You are my color orange,
that brings the best out of me,
that carves me the best out of me.
You are my color orange,
that makes me the happiest color of me.

Dreams on hold

Dreams;
that shattered with the ring of alarm tone,
Dreams;
that were jinxed before they were known,
Dreams;
that were a part of me, they were disown,
Dreams;
that defined me, that refined me,
Dreams;
that carved me, that shaped me,
Dreams;
that made in believe in love,
Dreams;
that made in mad in love,
Dreams;
that made me bloom in love.
Dreams;
that made me love who I am,

The first flight

On my first flight,
that scratched away unconditional love,
I left connections that were made with
delicate threads,
and with every mile,
they shred an inch of my skin,
and
then made pacts to be through thick and thin,
The connections were tangled with souls,
I knew it won't break with distance
we are each other's "kadak chai" for instance,
I knew I would need an over flown spoon of
patience,
with the right people at the right time and
these philosophies may seem nonsense,
but with time,
we learn, we unlearn,
we yearn for love.

Life goes on

Life goes on,

and

no plan works,

so

sit back and relax,

and

get on board with me,

so

I know you don't trust impulsive decisions

and

its fair,

so

why would you believe me,

and

what's there in store for you,

so

life is all about randomness,

and

random decisions brings out the best of you,

so

did that convince you,

and

if not, Life is a blend of unfinished stories,

let's not make ours add to it,
let's finish our stories,
our journeys,
our adventures,
on our terms.

Unfinished

13

Unfinished;
stories,
conversations,
journeys,
relations,
Unfinished;
books,
coffee,
journals,
rain,
Unfinished;
Me,
You,
They,
Them.

My first, My last

My first, My last,
In the eras of pacing and running after glitter,
You, my constant make my heart flutter,
As the miles mushroomed,
we as soulmates bloomed,
we were meant to be each other's happy place,
in the most embarrassing places, be each
other's grace,
You let me walk in your footsteps,
so that I don't stumble,
You shield me so that I don't crumble,
And let me hold your hand even though you
despise,
You are the brightest sparkle in my skies,
I admire you twice each second,
you take the wrath of heat to melt away my
worries,
You will always be in my forever stories.

Scars to stars

You made stars beneath my scars,
being beyond perfect, you raised the bar,
You faded my scars,
you faded my sorrows,
You shaded pink
to my scars,
you shaded love
to my scars,
you shaded joy,
to my scars,
you shaded happiness,
to my scars,
you were the light,
to my scars,
you were the life,
to my scars,
you were the shine,
to my scars,
you made me smile.
From scars to stars.

Forever, I will be there for you.

Forever,
I will be there for you,
You were there for me,
like sunshine on flowers,
like rain on barren lands,
like a cold gush of wind on sunny days,
like colored leaves in falls,
Forever,
I will be there for you,
You were there for me,
like a warm cup of tea,
like a warm hug to cry,
like a sweet treat to my life,
you cheered for me,
you cried for me,
you lived for me,
Forever,
you are mine,
I will be there for you.

Dear Amma

An epitome of simplicity,
carved with true beauty,
holds unconditional love,
love with no bounds,
no limits,
The love which is pure,
which holds every cure,
The warmth that melts all cold hearts,
The strength that shakes all rigid hearts,
The sacrifices often unnoticed,
The efforts often unbothered,
we all take her love for granted,
I am guilty,
I miss her,
I took her love, her care, her for granted,
as if It was only she wanted,
but, I promise,
I will cherish,
I will admire,
I will fulfill all her desires.

A letter to me

In the era of double taps,
True insight has gone far away,
It's a place where I'm surrounded,
Unknown to self, I'm grounded,
The flashes of fake lives,
In which I too took a dive,
Unnecessary people and their opinion,
Where a genuine one is once in a million,
In the trivia of being social,
Give yourself a proposal,
To always look after you,
Even when there is no clue,
To find yourself in the dark,
Vaping the dullness and add a spark,
You, yes you, look after you,
When no one is there, be there for you.

What if

What if a day comes,
With no warning,
With no clue,
And I disappear out of the blue,
No matter how hard I scream,
No one will hear me like a dream,
There is no space to repent,
It was a lie the life I spent,
All my life was concerned about others,
No matter what I wanted, it was always to
please others,
Now that I am gone,
I am just an epitome,
That will soon fade away,
No matter how hard I try I can't stay,
I tried, I tried, I tried and failed
But still, I didn't stop, I sailed.

An open-book

I'm an open-book,
Often mistook,
On the verge of crack,
No one to back,
Yet I smile,
For a while,
They think,
I will sink,
Or
Maybe,
I will rise,
To their surprise,
Staying low,
Taking it slow,
I won't quit,
Not for a bit,
Stronger than ever,
Will fight forever.

Long distance

From
"hate you"
to
"lifelines"
From
"unbothered"
to
"concerned"
From
"unseen"
to
"long calls"
From
"no sharing"
to
"caring"
"us"
siblings
grew
up.

Mindful

To the beautiful evenings shared,
To the evening teas,
To the silly gossip,
To endless bickers,
To screaming your lungs out during
blackouts,
To walk to each other's rooms using flashes,
To last-moment runs,
To last-moment practicums,
To last-moment lunch plans,
To eat each other's lunch boxes,
To making weird food recipes,
To celebrate birthdays in hostels,
To the uncertain endings,
To be with each other forever,
To walk past each other as strangers.

Once more

Life is golden,
Its once in a lifetime chance,
Lets make the best decisions,
and the opportunities that we were devoid of,
lets create them
"ONCE MORE"